500 DRAWING PROMPTS

Can You Draw It?

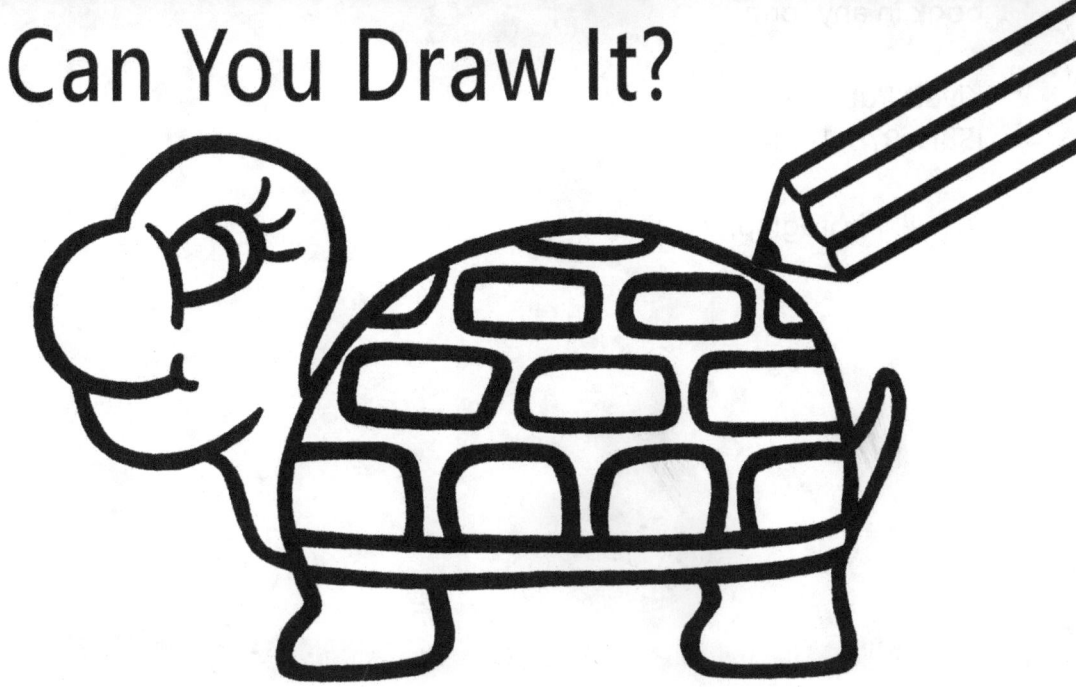

Jenny Pearson

500 Drawing Prompts
Can You Draw It?
Challenge Your Artistic Skills

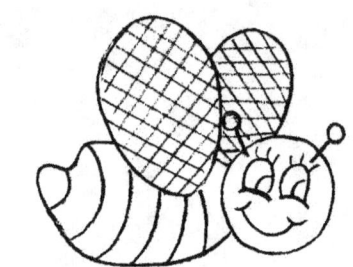

Kivett Publishing
ISBN: 978-1-534-88344-4

Arts & Photography > Drawing

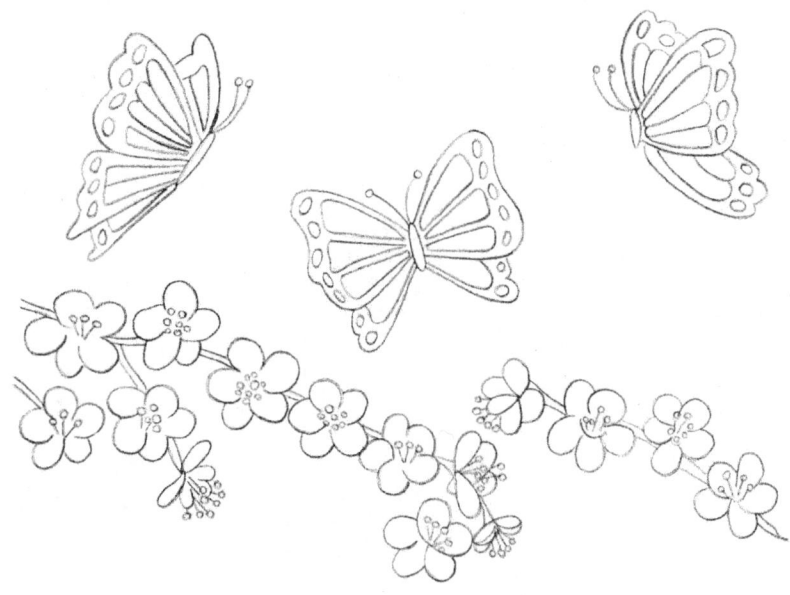

INTRODUCTION

Challenge yourself to draw 500 different images, from a butterfly to a winter scene.

How you choose to draw is up to you:
- the way it looks to your eye
- with artistic license
- comically
- abstract representation

The choice is yours. Put your creativity to the test.

1 Butterfly

3 Beetle

2 Bumblebee

4 Grasshopper

5 Rose

7 Sunflower

6 Tulip

8 Iris

9 Cat

11 Dog

10 Kitten

12 Puppy

13 Apple

15 Strawberry

14 Banana

16 Watermelon

17 Eye

19 Mouth

18 Ear

20 Nose

21 Triangle design

23 Circle design

22 Square design

24 Oval design

25 Sun

27 Cloud

26 Moon

28 Rainbow

29 Hand

31 Arm

30 Foot

32 Leg

33 Scissors

35 Gift box

34 Pencil

36 Sunglasses

37 Diamond

39 Hexagon design

38 Pentagon design

40 Octagon design

41 Giraffe

43 Tiger

42 Elephant

44 Zebra

45 Corn

47 Broccoli

46 Carrot

48 Head of lettuce

49 Face

51 Man

50 Body

52 Woman

53 Happy

55 Fun

54 Sad

56 Bored

57 Star

59 Heart

58 Crescent

60 Clover

61 Drum

63 Guitar

62 Harp

64 Piano

65 Frog

67 Duck

66 Horse

68 Snake

69 Strength

71 Determination

70 Courage

72 Motivation

73 Waffle

75 Hot dog

74 Ice-cream

76 Coffee mug

77 Socks

79 Pants

78 Shoes

80 Shirt

81 Smile

83 Pout

82 Frown

84 Smirk

85 Toaster

87 Television

86 Refrigerator

88 Sofa

89 Skunk

91 Shark

90 Turtle

92 Octopus

93 Fast

95 Hot

94 Slow

96 Cold

97 Lasso

99 Umbrella

98 Knot

100 Snowflake

101 Chair

103 Lamp

102 Table

104 Stool

105 Running

107 Rolling

106 Bouncing

108 Falling

109 Hammer

111 Wrench

110 Screw

112 Screwdriver

113 Car

115 Sailboat

114 Airplane

116 Train

117 Baby

119 Teenager

118 Child

120 Senior citizen

121 Cube

123 Sphere

122 Cube in perspective

124 Pyramid

125 Superhero

127 Villain

126 Superpower

128 Evil lair

129 Wind

131 Snow

130 Rain

132 Lightning

133 Christmas tree

135 Jack o'lantern

134 Valentine

136 Snowman

137 Hat

139 Belt

138 Tie

140 Suit

141 Shadow

143 Perspective

142 Gradient

144 Blurry

145 Flowers

147 Bush

146 Tree

148 Ivy

149 Ring

151 Bracelet

150 Earring

152 Necklace

153 Cylinder

155 Donut

154 Cone

156 Hourglass

157 Sparkles

159 Fire

158 Magic

160 Shiny

161 Golf ball

163 Hockey stick

162 Baseball

164 Hoop and net

165 Alien

167 Bigfoot

166 Spaceship

168 Monster

169 Dress

171 Blouse

170 Skirt

172 Jacket

173 Astronaut

175 Doctor

174 Fireman

176 Teacher

177 Checkers

179 Playing Card

178 Chess piece

180 Blocks

181 Bricks

183 Wood grain

182 Tiles

184 Wallpaper

185 Good

187 Victory

186 Evil

188 Defeat

189 Calculator

191 Laptop

190 Cell phone

192 Computer

193 Volleyball

195 Soccer ball

194 Volleyball net

196 Soccer goal

197 Button

199 Lock and key

198 Zipper

200 Nut and bolt

201 Hummingbird

203 Penguin

202 Parrot

204 Peacock

205 Water

207 Steam

206 Ice

208 Fog

209 Fire hydrant

211 Well

210 Windmill

212 Lighthouse

213 Love

215 Sadness

214 Anger

216 Laughter

217 Wallet

219 Backpack

218 Purse

220 Luggage

221 Monkey

223 Kangaroo

222 Lion

224 Rhinoceros

225 Angel

227 Fairy

226 Devil

228 Genie

229 Chimney

231 Deck

230 Fireplace

232 Pool

233 Ping pong

235 Skates

234 Billiards

236 Miniature golf

237 Short

239 Thin

238 Tall

240 Wide

241 Slide

243 Rock wall

242 Swing

244 Monkey bars

245 Tennis

247 Golf

246 Bowling

248 Baseball

249 Santa Claus

251 Cupid

250 Tooth fairy

252 Easter bunny

253 Muffin

255 Cookies

254 Chips

256 Candy

257 Police car

259 Ambulance

258 Fire engine

260 Tank

261 Inside

263 Upside down

262 Outside

264 Backwards

265 Dominoes

267 Marbles

266 Puzzle pieces

268 Jacks

269 Leaf

271 Branch

270 Twig

272 Stump

273 Kiss

275 Handshake

274 Hug

276 Slap

277 Camel

279 Fox

278 Lion

280 Deer

281 Curtains

283 Carpet

282 Blinds

284 Doormat

285 Toast

287 Steak

286 Potato

288 Salad

289 Teeth

291 Fingernails

290 Hair

292 Brain

293 Go

295 Wait

294 Stop

296 Hurry

297 Lake

299 Desert

298 Mountain

300 Jungle

301 Asteroid

303 Meteorite

302 Comet

304 Shooting star

305 Loud

307 Busy

306 Quiet

308 Relaxing

309 Ghost

311 Mummy

310 Witch

312 Skeleton

313 Peanut

315 Soup

314 Pretzel

316 Sandwich

317 Music

319 Song

318 Dance

320 Radio

321 Bikini

323 Snorkel

322 Swimming trunks

324 Flippers

325 Penny

327 Dime

326 Nickel

328 Quarter

329 Homerun

331 Hole-in-one

330 Touchdown

332 Goal

333 Gemstone

335 Treasure map

334 Gold coin

336 Treasure chest

337 Cow

339 Sheep

338 Goat

340 Chicken

341 Mustache

343 Sideburns

342 Beard

344 Pony tail

345 Distance

347 Speed

346 Time

348 Acceleration

90

345 Distance

347 Speed

346 Time

348 Acceleration

90

349 Striped shirt

351 Plaid jacket

350 Polka dot shorts

352 Floral dress

353 Lizard

355 Raccoon

354 Crocodile

356 Bear

357 Picnic basket

359 Barbecue

358 Picnic blanket

360 Park bench

361 Desire

363 Confidence

362 Greed

364 Jealousy

365 Nest

367 Anthill

366 Doghouse

368 Honeycomb

369 Ladder

371 Escalator

370 Staircase

372 Elevator

373 Salt and pepper

375 Hot and cold

374 Peanut butter and jelly

376 Earth and moon

377 Logo

379 Billboard

378 Sign

380 Advertisement

381 Wheel

383 Gears

382 Lever

384 Pulley

385 Candle

387 Torch

386 Lantern

388 Searchlight

389 Rattle

391 High chair

390 Pacifier

392 Crib

393 Ant

395 Dragonfly

394 Mosquito

396 Centipede

397 Snap

399 Stomp

398 Clap

400 Whistle

401 Hammock

403 Wave

402 Beach

404 Sunset

405 Fence

407 Wall

406 Gate

408 Hedge

409 Milk

411 Juice

410 Soda

412 To go cup

413 Square peg, round hole

415 Early bird gets the worm

414 Up a creek without a paddle

416 Mind over matter

417 Fan

419 Parachute

418 Kite

420 Whirlwind

421 Near

423 Old

422 Far

424 New

425 Bride

427 Bouquet

426 Groom

428 Wedding cake

429 Prism

431 Magnifying glass

430 Lens

432 Telescope

433 Surfboard

435 Raft

434 Canoe

436 Lifeboat

437 Gloves

439 Robe

438 Boots

440 Earmuffs

441 Bacon

443 Grapes

442 Butter

444 Mushroom

445 Fist

447 Thumbs up

446 Fingers crossed

448 Thumbs down

449 Poodle

451 Bloodhound

450 Dalmation

452 Bulldog

453 Tent

455 Canteen

454 Sleeping bag

456 Campfire

457 Math

459 Art

458 Science

460 History

461 Army

463 Marines

462 Navy

464 Air force

465 Island

467 Canyon

466 Peninsula

468 Plateau

469 Luck

471 Character

470 Wisdom

472 Power

473 Dragon

475 Princess

474 Knight

476 Castle

477 Beaver

479 Pig

478 Goose

480 Rooster

481 Clown

483 Tightrope walker

482 Juggler

484 Trapeze artist

485 Asleep

487 Surprised

486 Yawn

488 Tears

489 Elf

491 Goblin

490 Dwarf

492 Troll

493 Reflection in a mirror

495 Funhouse mirror

494 Reflection in water

496 Rearview mirror

497 Spring

499 Autumn

498 Summer

500 Winter

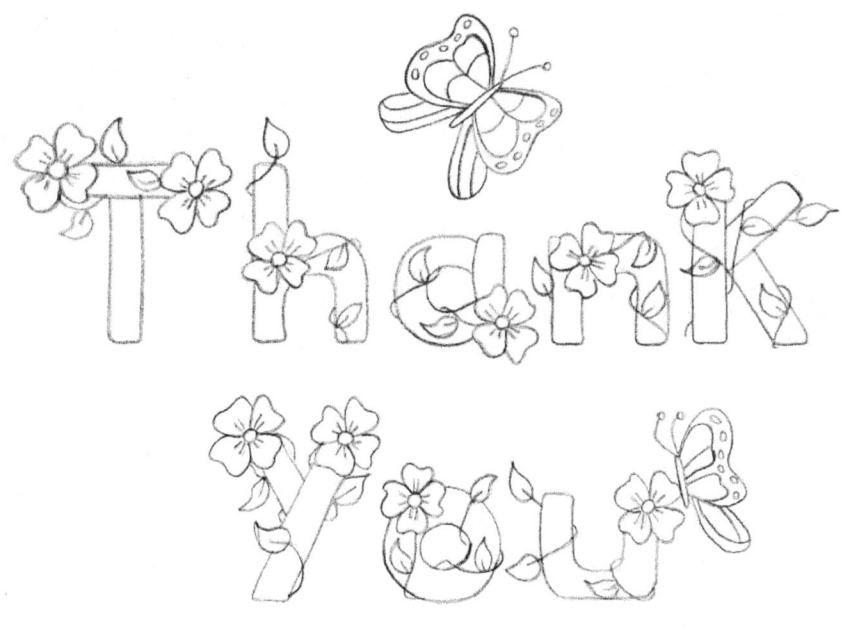